Portrait of
WASHINGTON

 *Portrait of America Series*

Portrait of
WASHINGTON

Photography by Ray Atkeson
Text by Tom Barr

GRAPHIC ARTS CENTER PUBLISHING COMPANY
Portland, Oregon

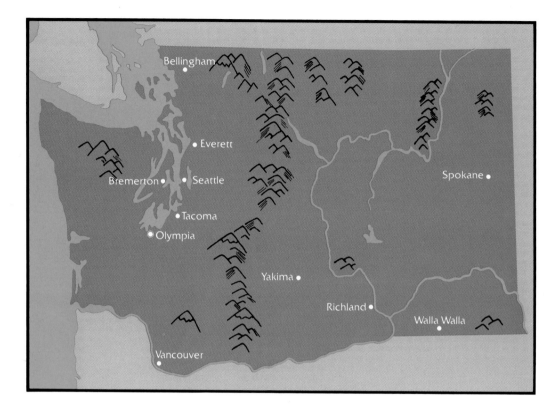

Cover: *Autumn foliage reflects across the waters of Trout Lake Creek in southern Washington.*

Title Page: *After plunging over Eagle Falls, the Skykomish River becomes a torrent in this narrow granite gorge on the western slope of the Cascades.*

Acknowledgments: *Photographs on pages 16, 32, 34 and 38 by Russell Lamb.*

International Standard Book Number 0-912856-53-X
Library of Congress catalog number 79-55977
Copyright © 1980 by Graphic Arts Center Publishing Company
P.O. Box 10306, Portland, Oregon 97210
(503) 226-2402
Typesetting • Paul O. Giesey / Adcrafters
Printing • Graphic Arts Center
Binding • Lincoln & Allen
Printed in the United States of America
Revised Edition, 1983
Third Printing

Contents

The Olympics and Southwestern Washington

White men first looked at the future state of Washington from the decks of ships. The Spanish came first, in 1774, with Bruno Heceta — the first white man to land—arriving a year later. One story, probably apocryphal, says that a Greek seafarer named Juan de Fuca reached these shores in 1592, giving his name to the strait that separates the Olympic Peninsula from Vancouver Island, British Columbia. However, history seems to accept that an Englishman, Captain Barkley, discovered the strait in 1787 and named it after the legendary explorer.

England followed on the heels of Spain. In 1778, Captain James Cook sailed along this coast on his third and last voyage. In a spell of bad weather, he passed the mouth of the Columbia River without noticing it, named Cape Flattery on the Olympic Peninsula's northwesternmost tip, and sailed on to Alaska. In 1788, Captain John Meares entered the mouth of the Columbia in dense fog and mistook it for a large inlet. He named the entrance Deception Bay and the cape north of the river Disappointment.

On April 29, 1792, two English ships, *H.M.S. Discovery* and *Chatham*, met the American merchant ship *Columbia* off the northern coast of the Olympic Peninsula. The English captain, George Vancouver, and the American captain, one-eyed Robert Gray of Boston, were searching—like many before them—for an eastward passage to the Great Lakes. After exchanging information, each steered an independent course into history.

Vancouver sailed the 85-mile width of the promontory and entered Puget Sound, the great inland sea that separates the Olympic Peninsula from the rest of Washington. Gray moved south, and some 100 miles down the coast he found the large natural harbor that now bears his name. But his greatest discovery lay ahead. Rounding Cape Disappointment, he entered a great river, which he named after his ship—the *Columbia*.

At the end of the eighteenth century, the flags of four nations were flying over the future state of Washington. England, Spain, Russia, and the United States all claimed the "Oregon country"—a vast region that included the present states of Washington, Oregon, Idaho, parts of Montana and Wyoming, and the province of British Columbia in Canada.

When Meriwether Lewis and William Clark crossed the continent in 1805-06, they entered Washington from Idaho by the Snake River. Completing their journey on the Columbia, they first viewed the Pacific Ocean from the headlands of Cape Disappointment. Their feat had both political and economic significance, for it strengthened the U.S. claim to the Northwest immensely and provided a route for overland fur trading.

Beginning in 1810, England and the United States engaged in fierce competition over the lucrative fur trade. After Spain relinquished her claims in 1819 and Russia withdrew hers in 1844, England and the United States occupied the Oregon territory jointly until 1846, with English settlements dominating north of the Columbia River.

The United States extended territorial government to this region in 1848 and made Washington a separate territory in 1853. Although it did not become a state until 1889, Washington assumed its present roughly rectangular shape in 1863, with the Pacific Ocean as its western boundary.

About one hundred miles inland the Cascade Mountains, stretching from the Canadian border to the Oregon border, act as a weather barrier and divide the state into a rain-blessed western sector and a relatively barren eastern plateau. Puget Sound bites into the northwest corner of the state, adding miles of shoreline, while the Columbia River forms three-quarters of the southern boundary and, with its tributaries, dominates the interior. These features divide the state rather easily into distinct regions — the Olympic Peninsula and southwest coast, the Puget Sound basin, the Cascades, and eastern Washington.

The harbor at Port Angeles on the northern edge of the Olympic Peninsula was discovered in 1791 by Captain Francisco Eliza, who explored the Washington coast for the Viceroy of Mexico. He called the four-mile sand spit the Port of Our Lady of the Angels. Through the years, the name was shortened to Port Angeles, and the community became the peninsula's largest city.

Thousands of vacationers know Port Angeles as the headquarters of Olympic National Park. Spread over 901,216 acres, the park covers one-fourth of the Olympic Peninsula, embracing all of the Olympic Mountains (part of the Coast Range), sixty glaciers, and a fifty-mile strip of seashore.

Left: At the base of Rocky Brook Falls, on the Olympic Peninsula, the water breaks into a silvery fan.

The park's highest peak, Mount Olympus (7,965 feet) receives 140 to 200 inches of rain each year, making it the wettest spot in the lower 48 states. Sequim, in the rain shadow 40 miles east of Mount Olympus, has an annual rainfall of 16 inches—the driest coastal region north of California.

From Cape Flattery south for 60 miles, there is no highway along the shore, and only one harbor within 100 miles. This is a coast for hiking and beachcombing, with driftwood to find and Japanese fishing floats to collect. You can even find rusting hulls and corroded anchors buried in the sand—memorials to those who died on these shores.

Just 15 miles below Cape Flattery, Cape Alava juts into the ocean, the westernmost point of land in the continental United States. Cape Alava is one of the western hemisphere's most important archaeological sites, for it has been occupied by man for at least 4,000 years.

South of the Olympic Peninsula, the Washington shore line is broken by Grays Harbor, Willapa Bay, and the mouth of the Columbia River.

By the early 1900s, the port on Grays Harbor, Aberdeen, was a rough lumberjack town, and its neighbor Hoquiam could boast of having one of the Pacific Coast's foremost timbermen, Robert F. Lytle, as a resident. His home—a magnificent example of turn-of-the-century opulence complete with ballroom, cut-glass chandeliers, antique furniture, and rosewood grand piano—has been restored and is open to visitors.

Today, Grays Harbor still shelters both timber awaiting export and fishing fleets. Hoquiam's factories produce chemical cellulose, and Aberdeen's industry centers around canneries.

Vacationers have been coming to Washington's southern coast since at least 1876, when stagecoaches carried passengers along the 28 miles of the Long Beach Peninsula. This long, thin promontory is separated from the mainland by Willapa Bay. Then as now, the waters off its shores offered superb salmon and tuna fishing, its beaches surf fishing for perch, sea bass, flounder, and halibut. The razor clam beds still attract diggers by the thousands, while others come to watch the 150 species of birds that gather annually at the Willapa National Wildlife Refuge. People who prefer other pastimes can stroll into the past on the peninsula's northern tip, where many houses date to the 1850s.

Seventy miles inland where the Columbia bends from north to west, are Longview and its sister city Kelso. As the first planned community in the Pacific Northwest, Longview has a history dating only to 1923. But for sheer volume of wood products output, it takes all honors.

Vancouver is the southwestern gateway to Washington and the state's oldest community. Though a thriving port, Vancouver is 100 miles from the sea. It sits across the Columbia River from Portland, Oregon, straddling Interstate 5, the main north-south freeway of western Washington.

Fort Vancouver was built by the Hudson's Bay Company in 1824 to strengthen England's claim to lands north of the Columbia River. Until 1846 (when Great Britain agreed to the 49th parallel as the boundary between Canada and the United States), this fort was the hub of the British commercial empire, which stretched from the Rockies to the Pacific and from Alaska to Mexican California.

In 1848 Fort Vancouver became the first U.S. Army post in the Pacific Northwest. When Ulysses S. Grant was quartermaster there in 1852 and 1853, he spent most of his time in Vancouver Barracks, the oldest building on the post.

When the original Fort Vancouver was excavated, it yielded approximately one million artifacts of stone, bone, pottery, and metal. Reconstructed as a national historical site and administered by the National Park Service, it lives on as a monument to the fur trade.

The Olympic Peninsula and southwest Washington contain many of the natural features and related industries that are found on a larger scale in the rest of the state. Although the terrain and climate are radically different, the loggers and dairy farmers of the Southwest interior and the dryland wheat ranchers and cattlemen of eastern Washington both court the productivity of the land. Fishermen along the coast share a vocation with those who work the waters of Puget Sound. Factories in Hoquiam, Vancouver, and Aberdeen have their counterparts in the industrial complexes of the Seattle-Tacoma area. The Olympic Mountains hint of the lofty grandeur of the Cascades, while the sprawling southwest timberlands are reminiscent of wide-open space on a much grander scale in the eastern desert country.

A small stream cuts channels in the sand of a coastal beach.

*Shadows of dune-grass dance across tracks left by a
bird on this southern coast beach.*

*Low tide exposes sea wrack, rockweed, and
eelgrass at Cape Flattery, on the northwest tip of the
Olympic Peninsula.*

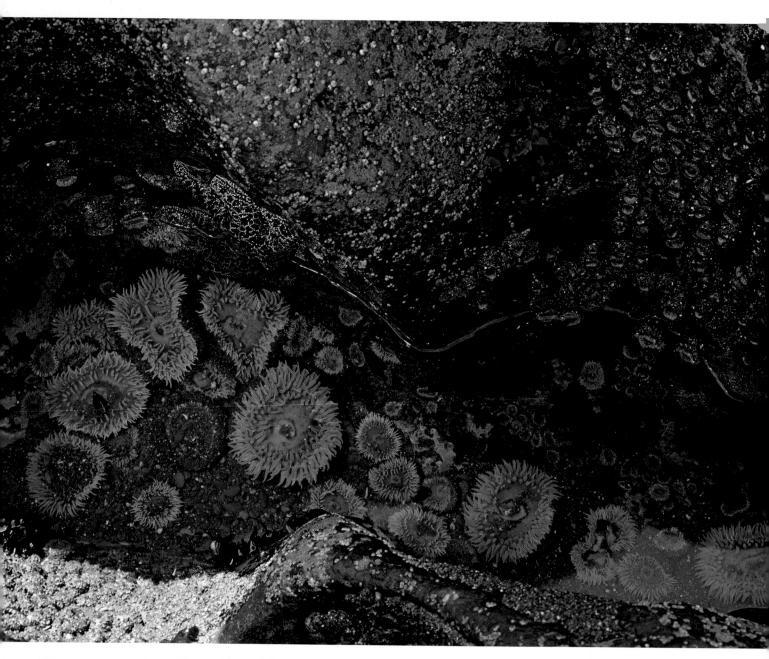

*Giant green anemones share a tidepool with a starfish
and other marine life on the north coast.*

Framed by the rugged shore of Cape Flattery, the lighthouse on Tatoosh Island marks the Pacific entrance to the Strait of Juan de Fuca.

North Head lighthouse, one of two near the Columbia River's treacherous mouth, began operation in 1898, and is now automated.

The quiet waters at Ilwaco, just within the mouth of the Columbia, have sheltered fishing boats for more than a century.

Hoquiam's Castle was built in 1897 by lumber tycoon Robert Lytle overlooking Grays Harbor, and is now listed in the National Landmark Registry.

Guarding the mouth of the Columbia, Cape Disappointment lighthouse marks the point from which Lewis and Clark in 1805 first viewed the Pacific.

Dense vegetation along the banks of the Dosewallips River attests to the heavy rainfall on the Olympic Peninsula.

The lovely avalanche fawn lily, with white petals and yellow center, bloom in early summer in the Olympic high country.

Overleaf: Soft green light gleams through moss-draped maple trees in the famous rain forest of Olympic National Park.

19

Cedar and spruce tower above a stream fringed with
vine maple in this land of dense forests and perpetual
moisture.

Mount Olympus, near the center of this Olympic range, is actually three peaks —East, Middle and South —the highest of which rises to 7,965 feet.

Shallow-rooted alder trees growing in the moist Hoh River Valley are quickly covered with thick moss once they fall.

Maple trees are hosts to selaginella and licorice fern
thirty to forty feet above the dense rain's floor.

Puget Sound

When Captain George Vancouver anchored his ships off Saltspring Island in 1792, he sent small boats out to explore the shorelines of the inland saltwater sea that he had reached through the Strait of Juan de Fuca. As was his custom, Vancouver set about naming landmarks in honor of expedition members, British naval officers, family, friends, and members of the royal family. He christened Washington's highest peak for Rear Admiral Peter Rainier; Mount Baker for his third lieutenant, who had been the first to see it; and the largest island for Joseph Whidbey, the *Discovery*'s master. The 100-mile-long inland sea he called Puget Sound in honor of his second lieutenant, Peter Puget, who had been in charge of the exploratory party.

After exploring for two days in the sound and before continuing north toward British Columbia, Vancouver wrote, "The serenity of the climate, the innumerable pleasing landscapes, and the abundant fertility that unassisted nature puts forth require only to be enriched by the industry of men ... to render it the most lovely countryside that can be imagined." Since then many people have agreed with Vancouver, for the Puget Sound basin has become the heartland of Washington.

The basin, a wide valley that drains the land between the Olympic and Cascade ranges, encircles the sound from the Canadian border on the north to Olympia on the south. Huge industrial complexes sprawl along the eastern shore and at the south end extend inland to the foot of the Cascades. Over two-thirds of the state's population lives in this corridor.

Olympia, designated the capital when the Washington Territory was formed in 1853, remained the seat of government after Washington was admitted as the forty-second state on November 11, 1889. Olympia's capitol building is unique in that the dome contains no steel reinforcements. It is one of the very few in the United States built entirely of stone masonry.

Port Townsend, 100 miles north of Olympia, overlooks Puget Sound from a promontory on the northeasternmost tip of the Olympic Peninsula. During the mid-19th century, the residents of Port Townsend harbored dreams that their town might become a great seaport or perhaps the seat of state government. But their dreams died when the railroads chose Seattle and Tacoma instead, leaving Port Townsend as a mill town and military post.

For several decades, the Victorian mansions and public buildings of Port Townsend rivaled San Francisco. Today tourists of all ages delight in these gaudy gingerbread pieces of the past as well as in the ring of forts that once guarded Puget Sound against invaders who never came.

Seattle lived in the shadows of Olympia and Port Townsend until July 17, 1898, the historic day when the steamer *Portland* docked at its waterfront. Sixty-eight miners debarked carrying sacks and suitcases filled, they said, with gold from the Yukon. A newspaper reporter, in a moment of imagination, announced that the *Portland* had "a ton of gold" aboard. Soon the rush was on, and Seattle boomed. More than 150 ships, schooners, barks, barges and floating death traps crowded into Puget Sound to take stampeders to the new El Dorado. During the next decade, over $200 million in gold floated through Seattle. About half of it remained, providing an economic base that has grown into the fourteenth largest market in the nation.

A population of 490,300 makes Seattle the largest city west of St. Louis and north of San Francisco. The home of Boeing Aircraft, it is a leader in aerospace and related industries. Shipyards, foundries, electronics, marine science, food processing, forest products, and natural gas refining are other major contributors to the economy.

The Port of Seattle is a multi-million-dollar municipal corporation encompassing 23 major waterfront terminals, a small boat marina for 1,550 craft, and a 700-boat commercial fishing terminal. More than 8,500 deep-sea commercial vessels from throughout the world berth at Seattle's harbor each year, carrying wheat, television sets, coconuts, bananas, cars, limestone, fertilizer, and molasses.

Southeast of Seattle are Renton, where Boeing manufactures commercial airliners, and Kent, whose 150 firms produce aerospace, communications, and computer equipment. Tacoma is the second major port on Puget Sound and Washington's third largest city, stretching from Seattle on the north virtually to Olympia, sixteen miles south.

The community of North Bend rests in the Cascade basin, 25 miles east of Seattle. Travelers on

Left: A wind-bent fir grows along the shore of Lopez Island, the third largest of more than 170 islands in the San Juan Archipelago.

Interstate 90, the major eastbound freeway, pass through North Bend on their way to the Snoqualmie Pass recreation area, eastern Washington, and Ellensburg. Many stop to see North Bend's premier tourist attraction — 268-foot Snoqualmie Falls.

North of Seattle lie the residential communities of Bellevue and Kirkland and the lumber port of Everett. From their outskirts open farmlands extend east to the Cascades and north to the British Columbia line. Whatcom County, which borders Canada, is Washington's leader in dairy products, poultry, strawberries, and raspberries. The city of Bellingham, 15 miles south of the border on Puget Sound, thrives with pulp and paper mills, several oil refineries, and a large commercial fishing fleet.

Washington has more than 2,000 miles of seashore along protected inland waters. One thousand of these miles border Puget Sound. The islands of the sound have secluded coves and beaches where one may dig clams, fish for salmon, and gather oysters and crabs. It is not surprising that boating and fishing lead the list of recreational pursuits in the state. There are twice as many boats per thousand people in Washington as in any other part of the nation.

In the northern waters of the sound, the 172 islands of the San Juan archipelago are scattered over 900 square miles of water from Washington's mainland to Vancouver Island. Many rise out of the sea in steep cliffs with boulder-strewn beaches at their base.

The quiet, pastoral San Juan Islands are favorites of salmon fishermen and yachtsmen. Although resorts dot Lopez, Orcas, and San Juan islands, many of the islands have permanent residents, too — farmers and former city dwellers who have forsaken the metropolitan pace.

These islands' serenity belies their often turbulent history. Discovered and named by the Spanish in the early 1770s, the San Juans were soon inhabited by British and American settlers, pirates, and smugglers. Wood, liquor, mutton, and Chinese immigrants were passed between Washington and Vancouver Island. Some cargoes never reached their destinations. Rip tides, reefs, rocks, and storms often brought shipwreck and death. You can still find rotting hulks along with occasional kegs of rum and other contraband.

Through the 1850s the islands were claimed by both the United States and Great Britain. When an American shot a pig belonging to a Hudson's Bay Company employee, the English demanded that he be tried in Victoria, British Columbia. American settlers were outraged. The United States sent troops to San Juan Island to maintain order. In March 1860, the British also sent a detachment. The "Pig War" lasted 12 years and may have been the friendliest conflict ever waged. Opposing forces entertained each other at elaborate dinners, athletic events, and in mutual celebration of national holidays.

When the fuss was finally arbitrated by Kaiser Wilhelm I of Germany in 1872, the islands were granted to the United States. San Juan Island, site of both encampments, has the distinction of being the last place in the territorial limits of the United States to fly the British flag. The reconstructed military base has been designated San Juan Island National Historical Park.

Whidbey Island, the second largest in the continental United States, is 46 miles long, with an irregular shoreline of pleasant coves and beaches. Most of its surface is rolling countryside, wooded hills, and berry farms. After World War I, grain, cattle, dairy, and poultry farming flourished here.

Coupeville, an old seaport on Whidbey, is Washington's largest registered historical district. The fort's gun emplacements and bunkers date to the 1890s, when it guarded the entrance to Puget Sound.

The Kitsap Peninsula and Bainbridge Island form a huge triangular foot that fills the horseshoe of Puget Sound west of Seattle. Like Whidbey Island, their fortunes are closely tied to the navy. The peninsula has been the home of the Bremerton Naval Shipyard since 1891. With more than 10,500 civilian personnel, it has become the largest naval installation in the Pacific Northwest and the third largest industrial employer in the state.

Separated from the mainland by the sound and from the Olympic Peninsula by the Hood Canal, the Kitsap promontory is often ablaze with color. In spring Washington's state flower, the rhododendron, lines the roadways. During the summer, wild rose and flowering dogwood brighten the countryside, and in the fall leaves turn scarlet, amber, and orange. Hood Canal, a fjord-like arm of water extending virtually the entire length of the Olympic range, has both sandy beaches and forest glens, making it a favorite of weekenders and vacationers.

Viewed from Vashon Island, Mount Rainier punctuates the horizon across Puget Sound; called Tahoma by the Indians, it was believed to be a dwelling place of the gods.

Standing 607 feet high, the Space Needle dominates
Seattle's skyline; on clear days both Mount Baker
near the Canadian border and Mount Adams near the
Oregon border are visible from its observation deck.

*East of Seattle, on Interstate 90, 4,000-foot Mount Si is a
traveler's first close-up view of the Cascades.*

*Lake Cushman, near Hoodsport on the Olympic
Peninsula, is easily accessible by road.*

The largest share of the nation's flower bulbs is grown in Washington, mostly here in the Puyallup Valley.

Port Townsend boasts an extensive collection of restored Victorian buildings; this roof turret is on the Starrett House, built in 1889.

Narrow Deception Pass creates a turbulent tidal channel between Whidbey and Fidalgo islands in northern Puget Sound.

*The block house at English Camp on San Juan Island
was built in 1860 as the result of a border dispute
between England and the United States.*

Pleasure boaters anchor in Fossil Bay at Sucia Islands in the San Juans with Mount Baker visible on the horizon.

The lighthouse on West Point, now a part of Discovery Park, still guides ships past this point on Puget Sound and into Seattle's Elliott Bay.

A boat cuts through the early morning tranquility of Lake Cavanaugh, a popular resort in the foothills east of Mount Vernon.

Port Madison's harbor, on the north end of Bainbridge Island, is only a short cruise across Puget Sound from Seattle.

*Like matchsticks in a random pattern, giant fir logs
await final processing in a Port Angeles mill.*

The Cascades

There was a time, according to Indian legend, when all of Washington was a flat lowland. Near the seashore, trees grew tall and straight and the ground was covered with sweet grass and flowers. But the interior country was parched and barren. Eventually the desert tribes became despondent and turned for help to their friend, the Ocean. He responded by sending his children, the Clouds and the Rain, to turn the desert into meadows and pasturelands. To hoard the life-giving waters, the desert dwellers dug Lake Chelan and other large trenches. The Ocean grew angry at their greed. He took earth and rocks from the northern coast and built a great wall the length of the countryside, forcing the people of the East to live forever in a dry and harsh land. The quarry from which the stone and land were taken filled with water and became Puget Sound. The barrier, which still keeps the rain from falling on the east, is the Cascade Mountains.

Unlike the Cascades of Oregon and California, which were formed by volcanism and glaciation, Washington's mountains were created by folding and uplifting of sedimentary rocks. Except for the highest peaks, which are extinct volcanoes, they are made of granite, gneiss, and schist. There are fossils of clams and oysters in these peaks, for prior to 10 million years ago Washington was flat and the mountains of today were once an ocean floor.

The Cascades make their own weather. Parts of western Washington receive more than 100 inches of rain per year. When the clouds reach the mountains, the moisture condenses and falls on western slopes as rain and snow. Excluding Alaska, Washington has more year-round snow than any other state in the nation. The Cascades contain 756 glaciers covering 103 square miles. These rivers of ice represent roughly 80 percent of all glacial areas in the United States. They are a vital source of drinking water, for approximately three-fourths of the world's fresh water is stored in glaciers.

But this monumental wedge of stone, 100 miles wide and from 6,000 to 9,000 feet high at the northern border, is more than an arbiter of climate or subject of legend. The Cascades provide majestic scenery that is visible from many locations — including two of Washington's three national parks. Several volcanic peaks dominate the landscape like silver towers atop a bluish-green fortress. There are

thousands of miles of hiking and ski trails. In the Cascade mid-section, between Snoqualmie and Stevens Pass, is the Alpine Lakes region containing hundreds of reservoirs ranging from tiny pools to miles of surface water. At the southern border, where the range tapers to 50 miles across and 3,000 feet in elevation, the Columbia River has cut through the mountains and created one of the most magnificent gorges on the continent.

Mount Rainier National Park is Washington's number one tourist attraction and outdoor recreation area. At 14,410 feet, "the Mountain" stands as an isolated cone 9,000 feet above the surrounding range. On a clear day, when its snowfields are often ringed by spectacular cloud halos, it is visible for over 100 miles.

Rainier is truly a mountain of epic proportions. It has the highest volcanic summit, the largest single-peak glacier system, and the largest and longest glaciers in the "lower forty-eight". There is far more ice on Mount Rainier than in all of Glacier National Park. Rainier Park's most popular area — Paradise Ranger Station — receives approximately 575 inches of snow per year. In 1972 the station recorded the greatest snowfall in the world with a record 93.5 inches in one storm. While most of the earth's glaciers have been retreating in recent years, Rainier's have been expanding and advancing downhill. Some move from 50 to 100 feet per year. Evidence of past glaciation too, can be found everywhere in cirques, baby-blue ice masses, and U-shaped valleys.

It was lava, however, not ice, that created Rainier. The last major volcanism occurred 2,000 years ago, and as recently as between 1820 and 1824 there may have been up to fourteen minor eruptions. Steam continues to melt tunnels in the summit ice cap. The Paradise River runs under the glacier to vast caverns with unusual ice-crystal coloring. Hikers have descended 400 feet below the surface.

In the foothills of this cold, austere world grows a community of 200-foot Douglas fir and trees of lesser heights such as western hemlock, red cedar, Pacific silver fir, and a 1,000-year-old stand of Sitka spruce. More than seven hundred species of wildflowers have made the park's meadows almost as famous as its glaciers. The first annual blooming usually occurs in July with the appearances of

Left: Edith Creek bubbles and splashes down the south slope of Mount Rainier (elevation 14,410 feet) near Paradise Inn and the Visitor Center in Mount Rainier National Park.

mountain buttercup, marsh marigold, and glacier lily, which pops up through the snow banks. A second flowering in August brings lupine, Indian paint brush, and a host of other blossoms.

With 40 glaciers covering 50 square miles, 34 waterfalls, and 62 lakes spread over 235,404 acres, Mount Rainier has become a favorite of hikers and mountain climbers. The rugged terrain offers virtually every climbing challenge in existence. Approximately 4,000 climbers reach Rainier's summit each year. Nature lovers have one hundred species of birds and sixty varieties of animals to watch.

North Cascades National Park, along the Canadian boundary, is divided into two units, plus the Ross Lake and Lake Chelan National Recreation areas. Dominated by the spectacular Picket Range and Eldorado Peak, North Cascades Park is nature's monument to the last great Ice Age. Within its 504,785 acres are hundreds of jagged, saw-toothed peaks, deeply glaciated canyons, snow hills, and 300 high-country glaciers. In this region of untamed wilderness and complex geology, walls of ice hang like shrouds and glaciers intermingle with ice aprons, icefalls, ice caps, waterfalls, and cascading streams. With its rough and rugged terrain, North Cascades Park offers some of the nation's finest mountaineering opportunities. The Cascade Crest Trail follows the summit of the range, and you can walk its length from Canada to the Columbia River Gorge.

In the southern section of the park, Lake Chelan of Indian legend cuts a 55-mile trough into the mountains. It is the deepest, largest, and longest natural lake in Washington. Looking up from the deck of a cruise boat, you can sometimes see mountain goats staring down from precipitous ledges. Although hunting is not permitted in national parks, it is allowed in national recreation areas such as Chelan.

Individual peaks, without parks, dominate other parts of Washington's Cascades. At 12,307 feet, Mount Adams in southern Washington, is the second highest peak in the Pacific Northwest. It sits in isolated splendor overlooking patches of alpine forest, open stretches of rimrock, and lava flows.

When nearby Mount Saint Helens erupted on May 18, 1980, it exchanged its well-known beauty for the even greater distinction of being the only active volcano in continental United States.

In the immediate area is Ape Cave, a huge tube formed when surface lava cooled while the molten material below continued to flow. The 11,000-foot tunnel that was left is the longest cave in the state. In this region where volcanism ran rampant, there is also a 12,500-acre lava flow and a deep crater.

Glacier Peak (10,541 feet) a favorite with mountain climbers, looks down on 30 smaller but equally rugged peaks in its surrounding wilderness. The views on the way to the top of Glacier are spectacular, and the potential for future climbing challenges must be endless. Although Mount Baker (10,778 feet) last erupted in 1854, the dormant volcano still emits sulfurous fumes. Scientists watch Rainier, Baker, and other peaks very closely, since Mount Saint Helens proved that the fire still burns down below and these volcanoes too could erupt again.

If in places the Cascades are a hunter's heaven and a climber's Eden, the range as a whole is a skier's paradise. Crystal Mountain features a 2,450-foot drop from a 6,800-foot peak and is so popular that it takes five double chairlifts, a triple chairlift, nine rope tows, and a T-bar to transport the hoardes of skiers up its slopes. Snoqualmie Pass, Washington's first commercial ski area, has more developed slopes than any other area in the state. North Cascades has no downhill runs, but it has become a favorite of cross-country enthusiasts. Stevens Pass and other areas have become meccas for both cross-country and downhill skiers and jumpers.

Stevens Pass became famous in 1929 with the completion of Cascade Tunnel, the longest railroad tunnel in North America. It runs under the pass for 7.8 miles and was one of the largest construction projects of its time.

In 1963 Leavenworth decked itself out in gabled roofs, gingerbread balconies, domes, and cupolas. The "Touch of Bavaria" theme won awards and continues to enchant visitors. Hosting the International Ski Jump Tournament has made Leavenworth one of the ski-jumping capitals of the West. Between winters, it bides its time by raising fruit and fish. Leavenworth was one of the first communities in the state to use irrigation, and it is the home of the nation's largest salmon hatchery.

"Mountains", said Nathaniel Hawthorne, "are the earth's undecaying monuments." They are artistry born of fire and ice, and refined by the etchings of wind, rain, and snow. Seldom has nature shown her artistry so magnificently as in the Cascades.

New fallen snow blankets the forest, and covers 12,307 foot Mount Adams, the state's second highest peak which has nine distinct glaciers on its sides.

Beyond Winchester Peak in the rolling North Cascades
stands lofty Mount Baker, a volcano dormant
since 1842.

*Vine maples like these near a vacant campsite in
Mount Baker National Forest, wear spectacular color as
autumn's days shorten and evenings become crisp
and cool.*

Trout Lake Creek, flowing here over a lava shelf, is one of the countless streams in the southern Cascades.

Rain-fed waterfalls are part of the ever-changing beauty found throughout the North Cascades.

Overleaf: The highest peak in North Cascades National Park, Mount Shuksan, reaches 9,127 feet; unlike many of the state's major peaks, it is not volcanic in origin.

Perfection Lake lies in the Enchantment Lakes Basin of the Stuart Range with Prusig Peak and The Temple rising behind it.

Table Mountain's square, flat summit is easily
recognizable, rising some 3,400 feet above the
Columbia River near Bonneville Dam.

*Deep, wet snow that completely cloaks the fir trees
and a lenticular cloud forming over Mount Baker turn
this winter landscape into a fantasyland.*

The floor of the Cascade forests are characteristically covered with lush vegetation, such as this vine maple growing among giant fir trees.

*Flowering stonecrop with its bright yellow blossoms
finds a satisfactory home in the cracks of a cliff in
Mount Rainier National Park.*

Mount Rainier reigns majestically over Cowlitz Box Canyon at the southern end of Mount Rainier National Park.

Steam rising from the lava dome of Mount St. Helens is
a reminder of the volcanic forces that altered both
Spirit Lake (foreground) and the mountain beginning in
March 1980.

The White Salmon River originates on Mount Adams and runs due south with much turbulance until it empties into the Columbia River.

Beneath Paradise Glacier, ice caves form and reform as warm air currents move through water-cut channels, each usually about two hundred yards long.

*Glacier-clad Mount Eldorado (8,868 feet) is in the South
Unit of North Cascades National Park, a four-section
park established in 1968.*

The Cascades are a rolling range of forested ridges and valleys punctuated with towering volcanoes such as recently reawakened Mount St. Helens and still dormant Mount Adams on the horizon.

In the southwest part of the state, before it empties into
the Columbia, the Lewis River becomes a stairway of
reservoirs, but here at its upper end, it flows freely.

East of the Cascades

Traveling east of the Cascade Mountains is like visiting a different country. The landscape is dramatically different from western Washington's. Mountains rise, not as walls of granite running the length of the state, but as isolated clusters of relatively low peaks. The Selkirk and Kettle Ranges fill the northeastern section with a jumble of crumpled topography. In the southeast corner, the Blue Mountains rise out of the surrounding wheat fields and spill into northeastern Oregon. The Boylston and Saddle Mountains lie east of the Cascades, between Yakima and Ellenburg, reaching like fingers into the flat lands of the Columbia Basin. Although few peaks in Eastern Washington exceed 6,000 feet in elevation, the Kettle Mountains' Sherman Pass, at 5,575 feet, is the highest pass in the state. Gone are the forests of Douglas fir and their thick undergrowth. The sweet grass meadows of the dairy lands are replaced by clumps of sparse brown bunch grass and fields of wheat that bend with the breeze and the natural roll of the land. People live differently, too. This is apple country — the nation's fruit bowl and the heart of the Inland Empire agricultural region. Cattle ranching is a $100 million-a-year business, and communities celebrate with rodeos and county fairs. The timber, commercial fishing, and aerospace industries, so important in the western portion of the state, are either of secondary importance or nonexistent.

Walla Walla, the Indians said, was the place of the "many waters," most of which ran off the western slopes of the nearby Blue Mountains. Situated six miles north of the Oregon border, Walla Walla today is surrounded by asparagus, onion, green pea and wheat fields.

During most of the 1800s, Walla Walla was one of the most famous settlements west of the Rocky Mountains. In 1818, Alexander Ross and Donald McKenzie of the British operated North West Company built Fort Nez Perce at Walla Walla. After the firm merged with the Hudson's Bay Company, the fort served as a supply base for both English and American interests. More important, America was able to claim joint occupancy of the Oregon Country with England.

In 1836, Dr. Marcus Whitman and his wife, Narcissa, came to Walla Walla with dreams of converting the Cayuse Indians to Christianity. Whitman built a mission, a grist mill, a sawmill, and a blacksmith shop and printed the first books in the Pacific Northwest.

On November 29, 1847, the Cayuse killed Whitman, his wife, and eleven others. The attack led to a war against the Cayuse and spurred Congress in 1848 to create the Oregon Territory, the first territorial government west of the Rockies.

Despite the Whitman Massacre, Walla Walla continued to grow. By 1859, it had the first bank, meat market, and Whitman College, which is the state's oldest institution of higher education.

In addition to Fort Walla Walla, the U.S. government built military outposts at Fort Spokane (east of the present Grand Coulee Dam) and Fort Simco, near Yakima. Despite a major Indian victory at Steptoe Battlefield, 33 miles south of Spokane, the Indians lost the war, and with it their lands. By the end of 1858 the last Indian campaigns were concluded.

The Spokane Indians were the "children of the sun," and the city that took their name has a bowl-like setting among pine-green hills and blue lakes. Spokane is now Washington's second largest city, and its location—165 miles east of the Cascades, 20 miles west of the Idaho border, and almost equidistant between Oregon and British Columbia — has been largely responsible for its prosperity. In the 1800s the settlement was the only point along a 400-mile wall of mountains where railroads could cross the Rockies and reach the Columbia Basin to the west. Today it is the hub of the Inland Empire— the vast agricultural region that includes half of eastern Washington and parts of Oregon, Idaho, western Montana, and southern British Columbia.

Between these two periods lumbermen, farmers, and mining companies built a business center of red brick on the banks of the Spokane River, which flows through the center of the city. When Spokane hosted Expo '74, the city was given a face lift that included Spokane River Park Center—an area along the river with outdoor theaters, an opera house, and a convention center, all surrounded by meadows.

Between the Cascade Mountains and the Idaho border, the communities and counties of eastern Washington spread in a semicircle from Spokane. Cut off from the moisture laden winds of the Pacific Ocean by the Cascades, they depend on the Columbia River for irrigation and power.

Left: A combine harvests wheat in the rolling Skyrocket Hills near Waitsburg in the fertile southeast, an area Lewis and Clark cut through on their return to Missouri.

From its headwaters in the Canadian Rockies, the Columbia flows for 1,270 miles before dumping 2,000,000 gallons of water per second into the Pacific Ocean. On the way, it drains 259,000 square miles of Canada and seven western states.

Throughout most of its history, the Columbia was a formidable river, swiftly flowing and filled with treacherous rapids. In the center of the state, the Columbia Basin is scarred with ancient coulees, or gorges, carved by the Ice Age river. Overflowing with glacial meltwaters, the river roared through the basin, plunging 400 feet over falls that were three and one-half miles wide. After the meltwaters drained away, the Columbia returned to its present streambed. The falls dried up, leaving an orange-red chasm as a serpentine skeleton of one of the greatest waterfalls in history.

While it is still the West's major salmon-producing stream, the Columbia no longer roars through Washington. Eleven dams have harnessed its energy and tapped its waters. The Columbia Basin Project has turned over one million acres of barren desert into fields of alfalfa, potatoes, sugar beets, corn, and a variety of seed crops.

The Columbia enters Washington in the northeast corner. For the first 150 miles southwest to Grand Coulee Dam, it is called Franklin D. Roosevelt Lake. East and west of the 98,500-acre Grand Coulee Recreation area are the Colville and Okanogan National Forests. The entire region is dotted with lakes, criss-crossed by streams and inhabited by few people. Colville National Forest, on the slopes of the Kettle Mountains, straddles Roosevelt Lake and is known for its record-sized mule deer, huckleberries, and mushrooms.

Grand Coulee Dam has been called man's greatest structure and one of his greatest engineering achievements. Set in the sweep of the eastern Washington desert, it is huge in every respect. Rising 550 feet from bedrock, 450 feet thick at the base, and 30 feet wide at the crest, the 4,173-foot-long dam produces a falls twice as high as Niagara.

From Grand Coulee, the Columbia swings in a wide arc south of the Okanogan country and near the Cascade foothills. After receiving water from Lake Chelan, the Columbia enters the Wenatchee and Yakima valleys before curving eastward toward the Tri-Cities area. After making a final loop around the Horse Heaven Hills at the Tri-Cities, the river completes its 300-mile journey to the Pacific Ocean as the Oregon-Washington border.

In 1856 Hiram Smith brought 1,200 apple trees by packhorse to the Okanogan Valley from Fort Hope, British Columbia. From his 24-acre orchard, Washington's apple industry was born. Irrigation was introduced in the Yakima Valley in the 1870s, and the fruit boom was underway. Today Washington grows more apples than any other state. Wenatchee ships 29,000 carloads annually and calls itself the Apple Capital of the World. Yakima, the Fruit Bowl of the Nation, 105 miles south of Wenatchee, markets peaches, pears, cherries, wine grapes, hops, tomatoes, and melons.

The economy of the Tri-Cities area is firmly linked to agribusiness and nuclear energy. In 1943 the desert hamlets of Richland, Kennewick, and Pasco were converted virtually overnight into modern cities with populations in the thousands. All the newcomers were employees of the U.S. Atomic Energy Commission's Hanford Project. The project was a by-product of Bonneville and Grand Coulee dams and the Columbia River. The dams produced abundant power, and the Columbia provided an inexhaustible supply of cold water, both of which were critical to the success of the Hanford project.

From the Tri-Cities area 65 miles northeast to Ritzville and 30 miles east to Walla Walla, the landscape is filled with seas of wheat, for the rolling Palouse country is one of the most productive grain areas in the nation.

Clarkston, on the Idaho border, is the jumping-off point for white-water enthusiasts. Here the Snake descends into a canyon 2,000 feet deep with sides of sheer basalt. It extends for 30 miles downriver to Lower Granite Dam. Little Goose, Lower Monumental, and Ice Harbor dams complete the Lower Snake River Project.

Forty species of fish are found in the Columbia and Snake, including white sturgeon, which grow to lengths of 20 feet and weights of 1,800 pounds. Fishermen work the lakes behind the dams and the calm pools in the river for bass, catfish, and salmon. About two million tons of freight move along the Snake every year, together with thousands of water skiers and pleasure craft.

Rabbit brush flaunts its fall bloom in an arid section east of the Cascades.

Late afternoon sunlight reflects the gold of larch trees on placid Thomas Lake, one of a small chain of lakes on the Little Pend Oreille, north of Spokane.

A barn in the Klickitat Valley stands serenely in the fading light of a winter afternoon, with cloud-capped Mount Adams in the distance.

The Wenatchee River —a popular river due to its
easy access by highway —picks up speed as it enters
Tumwater Canyon on the eastern slope of the Cascades.

The Palouse River drops 198 feet over a lava cliff at
Palouse Falls —downriver from the Palouse Hills
wheatlands, where fertile soil is worked by dry farming.

Overleaf: Built in 1941, Grand Coulee Dam is over
three-quarters of a mile long and 550 feet high, backing
up Franklin D. Roosevelt Lake for 150 miles.

A network of canals carrying Columbia River water
converted this once arid land into a patchwork of
irrigated fields.

Near Moses Lake, the Potholes Reservoir with its
countless sandy islands is popular with boaters and
campers.

The Columbia River flows past Northport, just south
of the Canadian border, before it reaches the still waters
of Lake Roosevelt.

Abandoned homesteads and ghost towns, are scattered throughout the Okanogan Region of northcentral Washington, many of which were built before the turn of the century.

Winter wheat crops utilize the volcanic soils and heavy
snowfalls of eastern Washington, turning the hills to a
deep green.

The Grand Ronde River Canyon is a steep, rugged area in the extreme southeast corner of the state, and is a tributary of the Snake River.

Aspen groves proliferate among the deep-green pine
forests of the high country; here a bough turns golden in
the autumn sun.